THE RIGHT TO DIE?

RICHARD WALKER

SEA-TO-SEA

Mankato Collingwood London

This edition first published in 2006 by
Sea-to-Sea Publications
1980 Lookout Drive
North Mankato
Minnesota 56003

Copyright © Sea-to-Sea Publications 2006

Printed in China

Library of Congress Cataloging-in-Publication Data

Walker, Richard, 1951-
   The right to die? / by Richard Walker.
      p. cm.
   Originally published: New York: Franklin Watts, 1997 (Viewpoints)
   Includes index.
   ISBN 1-932889-56-6
   1. Right to die—Juvenile literature. 2. Euthanasia—Juvenile literature. 3.Assisted
suicide—Juvenile literature. 4. Medical ethics—Juvenile literature. I. Title. II. Viewpoints
(Franklin Watts, inc.)

R726.W29 2005
179.7—dc22

                                        2004062517

9 8 7 6 5 4 3 2

Published by arrangement with the Watts Publishing Group Ltd, London

Picture acknowledgements:
The authors would like to thank the following for their permission to reproduce the
photographs included in this book:
Cover photograph: Science Photo Library/Mehau Kulyk.
AKG, London: "The Torments of Hell," Bibliothèque de Ste. Genevieve, 4T; "The Death of
Socrates," 1787, J.L. David, Metropolitan Museum of Art, New York, Wolfe Collection 10T ;
Andes Press Agency/Carlos Reyes: 5B, 19B
BBC: 13T; Bundesarchiv, Germany: 13BL
James Cant/Heaven on Earth, Bristol: 27BL
Mary Evans Picture Library: 6T, 8, 24B, 26B; Ponting 24T
Express & Star, Wolverhampton 28R
Robert Harding Picture Library: 7B, 28L
Hulton-Getty: 11L, 13BR
Hutchison Library: 26T; L. Taylor 25T
Magnum Photos Ltd.: Abbas 4B; B. Barbey 27T; P. Fusco 12; E. Richards 5T; C. Steele-
Perkins 19T
© McKlein Photos
Mirror Syndication International/Library of Congress: 9T
PA Photos/EPA 11R, 21T
Rex Features Ltd.: 20; T. Anderson 27BR; Kellas 6B; The Times 10B, 23T; Today 14, 16,
17TL, 17B
Rex Features Ltd./Sipa-Press: T. Baker 17TR; R. Falco 22
Frank Spooner Pictures/Gamma Liaison: Z.Kaluzny 25B;
B. Markel 15B; B. Mooar 9B; C. Vioujard 21B
Topham-Picturepoint Ltd.: 18, 29B.
Trip/H Rogers: 7T
Zefa: 15TL, 29T

Quotation credits, given from the top of a page beginning with the left-hand column:
p.4 1 Jean Jacques Rousseau, 18th-century French philosopher; 2 Kevin Toolis, the
Guardian newspaper, October 7, 1995
p.5 1 Woody Allen, American comedian, actor and film director (1935-);
2 Economist magazine
p.6 Walt Whitman, poet, at 70
p.7 1 Friedrich Nietzsche, 19th-century German philosopher; 2 Paula Hendrick, In
Context magazine; 3 Sir Ludovic Kennedy, President of the Voluntary Euthanasia
Society
p.8 1 Exodus 20:13, The Bible;
2 Genesis 1:27, The Bible; 3 Vatican's Declaration on Euthanasia, 1980;
4 Sura XVII 33, The Holy Koran
p.9 Ronald Dworkin, Life's Dominion: An Argument about Abortion and Euthanasia,
1993; 2 Malcom Muggeridge, journalist and social commentator, 1980
p.10 Seneca, 1st-century Roman philosopher and statesman
p.11 1 Sir William Blackstone, Commentaries on the Laws of England (1765-69); 2
Friedrich Nietzsche, 19th-century German philosopher; 3 Vatican's Declaration on
Euthanasia, 1980
p.12 1 Suicide Act of England and Wales, 1961; 2 Dr. Christiaan Barnard, pioneer

heart-transplant surgeon;
3 Information from ALERT, an anti-euthanasia organization
p. 13 1 Adolf Hitler, Mein Kampf, 1923
p.14 1 Ronald Dworkin, "The Right to Death," The New York Review of Books, January
31, 1991.
p.15 1 Bryan Appleyard, journalist, writing about Peter Singer, Professor of
Philosophy, Monash University, Melbourne, Australia, The Independent newspaper,
October 13, 1995; 2 Luke Gormally, The Linacre Centre, Euthanasia, Clinical Practice
and the Law, 1994; 3 Victoria Macdonald, journalist, Sunday Telegraph newspaper,
February 18, 1996
p.16 1 From the Hippocratic Oath, one of the bases of modern medical ethics; 2
Margery Caygill, in constant pain from chronic rheumatoid and osteoarthritis; 3 Sir
Robert Kilpatrick, President of the General Medical Council, November 1992
p.17 1 John Boyes, Lilian Boyes' son;
2 Dr. Robin Bernhoft, heading Washington Physicians Against (Pro-euthanasia)
Initiative 119, 1991; 3 Official Statement of the American Medical Association,
March 1996
p.18 Kathy Marks, journalist, the Daily Telegraph newspaper, December 2, 1995;
3 Husband speaking of his wife's final months in a hospice
p.19 1 Dame Cicely Saunders, founder of the modern hospice movement
p.20 1 Doctor's comment quoted by Richard Hare, Professor of Philosophy, University
of Florida; 2 Doctor magazine, April 1995; 3 Norra Macready, British Medical Journal,
March 1996
p.21 1 Voluntary Euthanasia Society Newsletter, January 1996
p.22 1 Extract from a living will; 2 Shane Snape, AIDS sufferer who completed a
living will, quoted in the Independent newspaper, July 1991; 3 Tony Blair, British Prime
Minister, 1997
p.23 1 Information from ALERT, an anti-euthanasia organization; 2 Paul Tully, The
Society for the Protection of the Unborn Child, during a BBC program ["Kilroy"]
March 7, 1995
p.24 1 Vatican's Declaration on Euthanasia, 1980; 2 Ronald Dworkin, source as p.9 2
p.25 1 Geoffrey Cannon, remembering his wife, Caroline Walker, who died from
cancer, The Good Fight: The Life and Work of Caroline Walker; 2 Walter Schwarz, the
Guardian newspaper, April 6, 1991
p.26 Tony Walter, Funerals and How to Improve Them
p.27 1 Nicholas Timmins, the Independent newpaper, January 31, 1996; 2 Sheila
Page, describing the experience of organizing the funeral of her terminally ill husband
before he died, Natural Death Handbook; 3 Walter Parsons, public relations officer for
the National Association of Funeral Directors, commenting on recyclable coffins, Time
Out magazine, October 30, 1991
p.28 1 Eric Dutson, AIDS sufferer in Oregon reflecting on the possibility of assisted
suicide becoming legal in that state, US News and World Report, December 19, 1994;
2 Sarah Kemp, from an interview with the BBC posted at www.news.bbc.co.uk,
19:9:03
p.29 1 Maureen Michaels, one of the only family in Britain signed up to be frozen at
death, quoted by Deborah Holder in Marie Claire magazine, 1995.

Contents

Death: the last taboo?

Death is the end of life. Together with birth, death is an event that all of us are guaranteed to experience, regardless of our race or social status. But unlike the other milestones in life, such as birthdays and weddings, we have no idea what death is like. Those who have experienced death are now dead, so we have no eyewitnesses to the event. It is hardly surprising, then, that through the ages the mystery of death has inspired much speculation and fear about its nature.

" He who pretends to look on death without fear lies. All men are afraid of dying, this is the great law of sentient beings, without which the entire human species would soon be destroyed. " Jean Jacques Rousseau, 18th-century French philosopher

To our ancestors death was very much part of life. Shorter life spans and high mortality rates during childhood meant that children were introduced to death at an early age. Dying, death, funerals, and mourning were all openly acknowledged and governed by tradition and ceremony. But while open attitudes to death survive today in countries such as

▶ *The Mexican Day of the Dead is celebrated on October 31 (Hallowe'en). It is a joyous occasion when the living, dressed in splendid costumes, remember the dead with dancing and parades.*

Mexico, the western world has apparently made death something to be hidden away and not to be talked about.

" Death shares with birth a unique status. It is both a universal and individual experience. Every human being in society will die, and yet death in the West is denied. It has become the ultimate taboo. " Kevin Toolis, journalist

Our conversations with others usually involve everyday matters such as vacations, friends, or music. How many of us regularly discuss death, or want to? If death is mentioned it is often dismissed in a flippant or humorous way.

▲ *Part of our fear of death stems from our ideas of what might happen after death—the belief in Heaven and Hell is ancient. This 15th-century French image shows the possible tortures of Hell.*

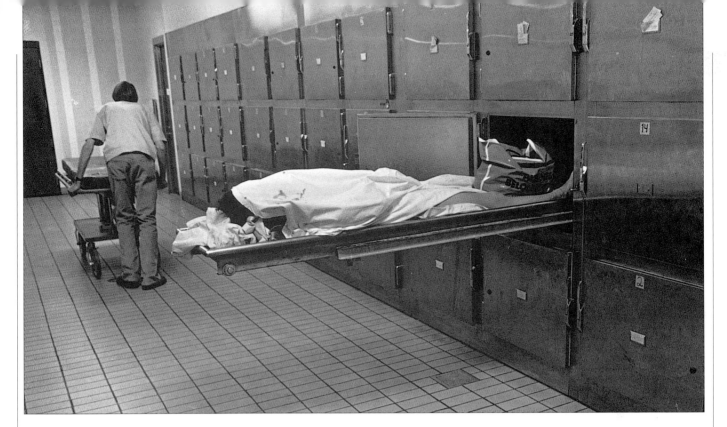

▲ *The body of a 14-year-old boy killed in an accident is put into cold storage in a hospital morgue. It will be picked up later by a funeral director, who will clean it and put it in a coffin.*

❝ *I'm not afraid to die. I just don't want to be there when it happens.* ❞ *Woody Allen, comedian, actor, and film director*

As health care has improved and the chances of us dying young have lessened, we have increasingly lost touch with death. Rather than seeing it as a natural event, we have come to view death in a negative sense, as a failure, or something that happens to other people. Dying and death have, in many cases, changed from being a family event to one that is

▶ *Some cultures are less inhibited about death than others. In Recife, Brazil, relatives and friends gather to express their feelings around the open coffin of a teenager whose body has been covered by flowers prior to burial.*

controlled and stage-managed by doctors and funeral directors. But does this mean that we have lost the right to control our death, in the same way that we control the rest of our life? Should death be the last taboo? Or do we need to open our eyes to all aspects of this important life event so that we can make informed decisions about it?

❝ *To civilize death, to bring it home and make it no longer a source of dread, is one of the great challenges of the age.... Gradually, dying may come to hold again the place it used to occupy in the midst of life: not a terror but a mystery so deep that man would no more wish to cheat himself of it than cheat himself of life.* ❞ *Economist magazine*

Longer, better lives?

Modern medicine and improved standards of public health, hygiene, and housing have transformed our lives. Until the beginning of the 20th century, many people had large families in the expectation that most of their children would die young. Today those of us living in the developed world not only expect our children to survive childhood but also hope that they will live on, as we hope for ourselves, into their 70s or 80s. Such aspirations would have been considered unrealistic by our Victorian ancestors. And they would

▲ This 17th-century portrait of the Remmington family of Yorkshire records Sir Thomas and Lady Hannah's 20 children: 15 are living but 5 are dead, indicated by the figures in white shrouds.

◀ Relaxing in a New York park, a man in his later years savors the delights of an old age made possible by improvements in health care.

have been astounded by the advances in medicine that allow us in the developed world to "cheat" death and live longer. But for most of us there is much to be said for living to a ripe, old age:

66 The old ship is not in a state to make many voyages, but the flag is still on the mast and I am still at the wheel. 99   Walt Whitman, poet, at the age of 70

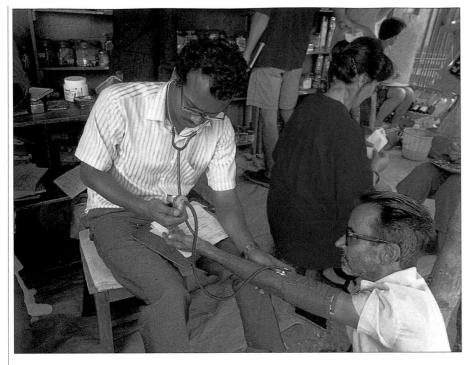

issues that surround it to the fore. In particular, demands for euthanasia to be legalized have increased:

66 *The whole question of euthanasia would be much less of a subject for topical discussion if it hadn't been for the enormous advance in medical science—the invention of drugs, the spare-part surgery—which has prolonged life far more than nature intended.* 99   *Sir Ludovic Kennedy, President of the Voluntary Euthanasia Society*

But increased longevity has generated its own problems. People in their later years may remain relatively healthy and well until they die. But as lives become longer, so do the chances of developing diseases such as cancer, which can result in long, debilitating, and painful illness. And modern medical care can prolong our lives still further while we suffer these illnesses.

66 *In a certain state it is indecent to live longer. To go on vegetating in cowardly dependence on physicians and machinations, after the meaning of life, the right to life, has been lost, ought to prompt a profound contempt in society.* 99
Friedrich Nietzsche, 19th-century German philosopher

While medical advances have undoubtedly improved much of our lives, they do force us to pose this question: Should we be able to reach

a "natural end" and die when we ought to die without medical intervention? Increasingly, many patients feel that they have lost control of their lives—and their deaths.

66 *We have become victims of the health-care system that our cultural values have created. The dying process has been transformed into a series of wrenching choices.... Out of the apparently needless suffering of countless people has grown a strong movement toward patients' rights and natural death—that is, death with a minimum of medical intervention.* 99
Paula Hendrick, In Context magazine

Medical advances have made us reconsider our whole relationship with death and brought the

Since our lives are sustained unnaturally by medicine, should we have the right to end them unnaturally, too?

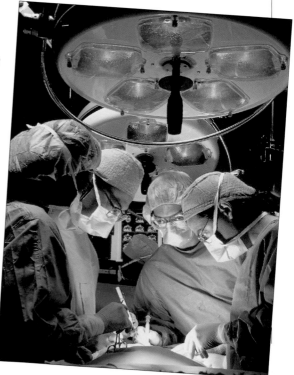

Is human life sacred?

We know, almost instinctively, that murder is the worst crime that any of us could commit. To do so would go against a belief that has underpinned human societies for thousands of years—the belief that human life is sacred.

66 *Thou shalt not kill.* **99**
Exodus 20:13, The Bible (The Sixth Commandment)

From the viewpoint of most religions, most notably expressed by the Roman Catholic Church, life is sacred and possesses an intrinsic dignity and value because humans were created by God.

66 *God created man in his own image.* **99** *Genesis 1:27, The Bible*

Each and every living human being is a representation on Earth of the Creator. During his or her lifetime, he or she is the possessor—but not the owner—of the God-given gift of life. For that reason, only God can dispose of the gift of life. Humans have no moral right to terminate their own life or the lives of others.

▶ *The great Hebrew prophet Moses descends from Mount Sinai to deliver the divine law of God—the Ten Commandments—carved in tablets of stone to his people during their flight from Egypt in the 13th century B.C. "Thou shalt not kill" was the sixth of these commandments.*

66 *Nothing and no one can in any way permit the killing of an innocent human being, whether…an old person or one suffering from an incurable disease.… Furthermore no one is permitted to ask for this act of killing, either for himself or herself… nor can he or she consent to it, either explicitly or implicitly, for it is a question of the violation of the divine law, a crime against life and an attack on humanity.* **99**
The Vatican's Declaration on Euthanasia, 1980

Some people believe there are two instances, however, where the principle of the sanctity of life does not apply and killing is "permissible": the capital punishment of a murderer; and the killing in warfare of unjust aggressors.

66 *Nor take life—which God has made sacred—except for just cause.* **99**
Sura XVII 33, The Holy Koran

Acknowledging that human life has an intrinsic dignity and value is not restricted to religious

believers. But there are many modern thinkers—both religious and secular—who are questioning whether a belief in the absolute sanctity of life is always appropriate: whether, when an individual's life is intolerable, perhaps because of pain, or close to its end, he or she should be permitted to seek release. Many feel that the most important part of our existence is not the fact that we are alive, but that we possess a quality of life.

66 People who want an early peaceful death for themselves or their relatives are not rejecting or denigrating the sanctity of life, on the contrary, they believe that a quicker death shows more respect for life than a protracted one. 99
Ronald Dworkin, Life's Dominion

However, this kind of attitude—that the individual should have control over his or her life and death—is anathema to those who hold a firm belief in life's sanctity.

66 Life is sacred because it is created by God for a purpose, and that purpose comes to an end when you die. It's not for you to choose the moment at which to die. 99
Malcolm Muggeridge (1903–90), journalist and social commentator

▲ Millions of soldiers died during World War I. Were their lives sacred? Or their deaths justifiable?

In discussing the right to die, your own viewpoint on the sacredness of life will play a large part in any conclusions you may reach.

▼ Paramedics in Washington D.C. endeavor to save a life by rushing their patient to the hospital.

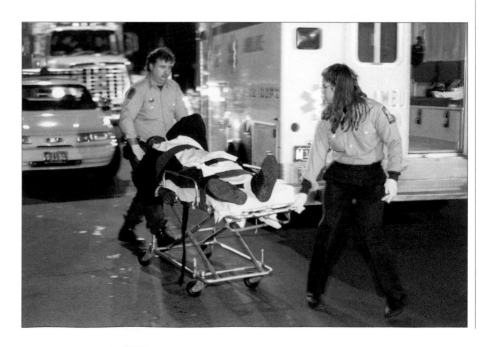

Can suicide be justified?

Suicide is the act of killing oneself intentionally. The act may be direct by, for example, taking a lethal substance; or indirect, by deliberately refusing life-sustaining treatment. But is suicide everyone's right? Or is it unlawful and morally wrong?

Historically, attitudes toward suicide have varied considerably. The ancient Greeks regarded suicide as acceptable in certain circumstances, as did the Romans. Both cultures believed that a good death was as important as a good life.

66 It makes a great difference whether a man is lengthening his life or his death. But if a body is useless for service, why should one not free the struggling soul? Perhaps one ought to do this a little before the debt is due, lest, when it falls due, he may be unable to perform the act. 99 Seneca, 1st-century Roman philosopher and statesman

Attitudes changed with the rise of Christianity. Suicide was seen as self-murder—a mortal sin because it contravened the doctrine of the sanctity of life. In some countries, the law reflected religion. In Britain, for example, suicide and attempted suicide were illegal until 1961.

▲ Greek philosopher Socrates killed himself in 399 B.C. by drinking a cup of the poison hemlock following his conviction for heresy in Athens.

▼ Chad Varah founded the Samaritans organization to provide a confidential and nonjudgmental befriending service for the despairing to contact.

▲ After months of illness, Nobel prize-winning author Ernest Hemingway committed suicide by turning his shotgun on himself on July 2, 1961.

66 *The suicide is guilty of a double offence: one spiritual, in invading the prerogative of the Almighty, and rushing into his immediate presence uncalled for; the other temporal, against the King, who hath an interest in the preservation of all his subjects.* 99 *Commentaries on the Laws of England (1765-69)*

But not everyone accepted the horrifying and sinful nature of suicide.

66 *The thought of suicide is a great source of comfort: with it a calm passage is to be made across many a dark night.* 99 *Friedrich Nietzsche, 19th-century German philosopher*

How is suicide viewed today? The Roman Catholic Church maintains the position that suicide is wrong.

66 *Intentionally causing one's own death, or suicide, is…equally as wrong as murder, such an action…is to be considered as a rejection of God's sovereignty and loving plan.* 99 *The Vatican's Declaration on Euthanasia, 1980*

This view is shared by many others, including nonbelievers, who see suicide as a sad and horrifying end to life, and few would disagree that there are many tragic suicide cases. But some regard suicide as an act of self-deliverance, a dignified and honorable means of release from mental or physical pain.

▲ Suicide can be used as a weapon and make a martyr of its performer. In 2003, a suicide bomber drove a truckload of explosives into the UN headquarters in Baghdad killing 23 people.

This argument is particularly relevant when a person is suffering from a terminal or long-term illness. Some choose suicide, but what if a person is so ill that direct suicide is impossible? Patients who are mentally competent have the right to refuse medical treatment, so causing their deaths, but what if they ask friends, relatives, or doctors to help them die by supplying drugs for them to take? This is assisted suicide, a form of euthanasia, and in most countries it is illegal.

Murder or mercy killing?

Euthanasia means literally "a good death": passive euthanasia is the withdrawal of a treatment that is keeping a patient alive; assisted suicide is another form of euthanasia; while active, or voluntary, euthanasia involves the intervention of a doctor to administer a lethal substance to kill the patient at his or her own request. The existing laws in most countries make practicing assisted suicide and voluntary euthanasia a crime.

▼ *A young man dying from AIDS. Would euthanasia give AIDS sufferers a "better death"?*

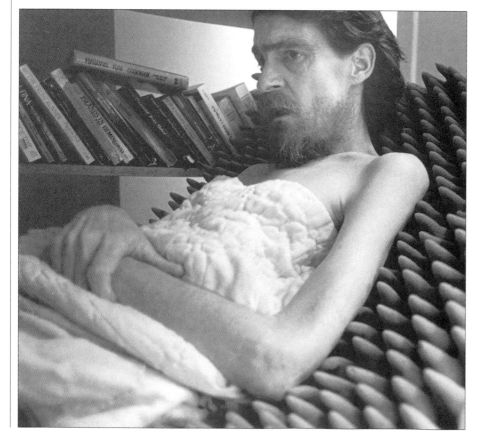

66 *A person who aids, abets, counsels, or procures the suicide of another, or an attempt by another to commit suicide, shall be liable on conviction on indictment to imprisonment for a term not exceeding fourteen years.* 99
Suicide Act of England and Wales, 1961

Voluntary euthanasia falls outside the suicide laws. A doctor who practices it can be prosecuted for murder. But many people feel that it is time for the law to be reviewed—The Netherlands and the Northern Territories in Australia have already

done so (see page 20). Euthanasia supporters believe that people with terminal and painful illnesses should be able to hasten their death with the help of their doctor.

66 *I have never seen any nobility in a patient's thrashing around all night in a sweat-soaked bed, trying to escape from the pain that torments him day and night…. To my mind, when the terminally ill patient has reached this stage, the best medical treatment is death.* 99 *Dr. Christiaan Barnard, pioneer heart-transplant surgeon*

While many people accept that doctors should not prolong the dying process indefinitely by providing unwanted care, there are those who see all forms of euthanasia as little more than legalized murder.

66 *ALERT defines euthanasia as 'any action or omission which is intended to end the life of a patient'. The law in every country until recent years has protected all citizens against being killed, regardless of their status or condition.* 99
Information from ALERT, an anti-euthanasia organization

Regardless of their viewpoint on the sanctity of life, many argue that the acceptance of any form of euthanasia could lead us down a "slippery slope" to involuntary euthanasia, the ending of a life without permission. As an example of this, they point to the mass "mercy killings" of thousands of people with physical and mental disabilities—*lebensunwerten Leben* ("life unworthy of life")—carried out in Nazi Germany before and during World War II.

66 *Society as a great authorized agent of life must be made responsible for every unsuccessful life—it has to pay for it, so it must prohibit it.* **99**
Adolf Hitler, Mein Kampf, 1923

The anti-euthanasia lobby argue that a change in the law could lead to a future where people would be "put down" simply because they were too old or disabled. Still others feel this is scaremongering and, given the correct legal framework, euthanasia

▼ A 1930s German poster informs the "German worker" that he carries the burden and cost of the "feeble-minded." Nazi philosophy promoted the ideal of "fitness" through groups such as the Hitler Youth (right).

provides the possibility of dying painlessly and with dignity. But is euthanasia necessary in an age when painkillers and advances in medicine can apparently take care of a patient's needs?

▲ Cees van Wendel de Joode (right) was a Dutch man who suffered from incurable motor neuron disease. He asked Dr. Wilfred van Oyen (left) to end his life. The documentary "Death on Request" recorded his last days and death by voluntary euthanasia. It provoked controversy around the world.

hier trägst Du mit
Ein Erbkranker kostet bis zur Erreichung des 60. Lebensjahres im Durchschnitt 50.000 RM.

A living death?

Many of the arguments about euthanasia focus on the aspect of patients' choice. However, some patients are unable to choose. Today, doctors can keep alive patients who are in a deep coma known as a persistent vegetative state (PVS) after suffering accidents or illness. The part of their brain that controls automatic functions such as breathing still works but the upper, "thinking," part of their brain shows no activity. Provided with food and water, patients with PVS can be kept alive, but is it right to do so?

66 Nothing in the idea that life has intrinsic importance…can justify a policy of keeping permanently comatose people alive. The worth of their lives—the character of the lives they have led—cannot be improved just by keeping the bodies they used to inhabit technically alive. 99
Ronald Dworkin, 'The Right to Death'

On April 15, 1989 a young soccer fan called Anthony Bland was crushed in a human stampede at the Hillsborough Stadium in Sheffield, England. His injuries left him in a

PVS, kept alive by feeding tubes. His parents and doctors felt that, with no hope of recovery, artificial feeding should be stopped. But feeding Anthony formed part of his medical care and by withdrawing it a doctor would be guilty of a criminal act. After a long legal battle, in which lawyers argued that passive euthanasia was in the patient's best interest, doctors were allowed to

▼ *Tributes to the 95 who died at Hillsborough. Tony Bland survived, but in a PVS; his parents had to live with the tragedy long after the event itself.*

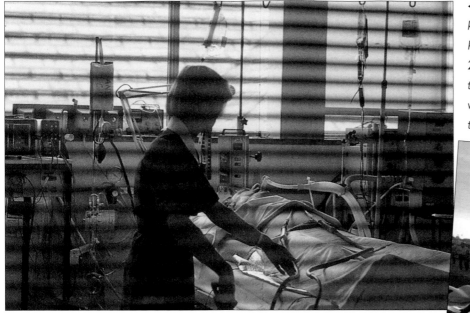

stop treating Anthony and he died in February 1993. It was a landmark decision.

66 We have come, he says, to the end of a 2000-year history of religious domination of morality. Under Christianity, human life from conception to death is sacred and unique.... The decision to let Bland die marked the end of that belief. 99 Peter Singer, Professor of Philosophy, Monash University, Melbourne, Australia, reported in the Independent newspaper

And it was questioned by those who opposed euthanasia and believed in the sanctity of life. They argue that the life of a patient with PVS has the same value and dignity as it did when the patient was fit and well.

66 PVS patients are living human beings, albeit gravely impaired. As living human beings they possess the inelimimable worth and dignity of our common humanity.... PVS patients are entitled to the ordinary care to which any impaired and vulnerable person is normally entitled. 99 Luke Gormally, the Linacre Centre

Fears about the removal of life support have also been raised by patients who have apparently regained consciousness after being in a PVS. One problem seems to be how precisely PVS can be diagnosed. Can it be distinguished from other states of deep coma in which patients do not respond, but from which they may recover?

66 Dr Keith Andrews at the Royal Hospital for Neuro-Disability, who led the study [into patients in PVS], said the findings were frightening. Over two years, 15 out of 80 patients thought to be in PVS came round. 99 Victoria Macdonald, journalist

Resolving this problem is one of the many dilemmas concerning dying that doctors have to face.

▼ "Right to die" cases in court attract a great deal of press attention. The parents of PVS victim Nancy Kruzan made several appeals to the U.S. courts over seven years before doctors were allowed to remove her life support.

A doctor's duty?

The role of any doctor is to care for her or his patients and, wherever possible, to keep them in good health.

66 *I swear…that I will prescribe treatment to the best of my ability and judgment for the good of the sick, and never for a harmful or illicit purpose. I will give no poisonous drug, even if asked to, nor make any such suggestion….* 99 *From the Hippocratic Oath, one of the bases of modern medical ethics*

But when a patient is dying, how should a doctor act to ensure the patient's best interests are taken care of? Should he or she listen to the wishes of the patient?

66 *What I would really like would be for a doctor to help me…. I know it would be done successfully…. I would like the help I would need to have a good death, as I'm trying to have a good life.* 99 *Margery Caygill, in constant pain from chronic rheumatoid- and osteo-arthritis*

Or should the doctor use all the medical resources available to keep the patient alive as long as possible?

66 *The public, rightly, need reassurance that they may expect their doctors to do their utmost to make a patient's death bearable and dignified, by easing pain and suffering. That is the doctor's duty. It is wholly outside that duty to shorten life in order to relieve suffering.* 99 *Sir Robert Kilpatrick, President of the General Medical Council, 1992*

Some doctors are moving away from this view. For example, one in seven British doctors have admitted to actively ending a patient's life, although a poll in 2003 found that 75 percent of the 986 British doctors surveyed would refuse to take part in an assisted suicide.

Doctors can be faced with appalling decisions. In the UK Lilian Boyes, a woman in extreme agony and very close to death asked her doctor, Nigel Cox, to end her life. He did so with an injection and was subsequently found guilty of attempted murder. However, he was given only a suspended sentence and was also allowed to continue practicing as a doctor. Lilian Boyes' family supported the decision.

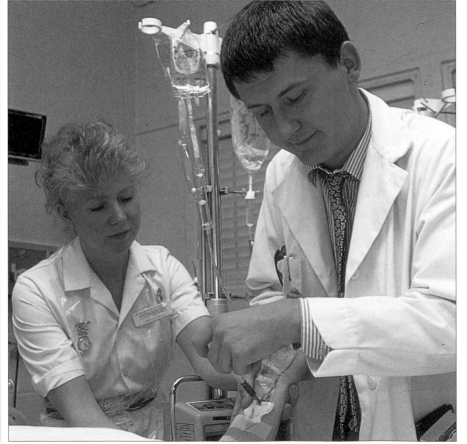

◀ A doctor treating a patient to the best of his ability to ensure a full recovery and good health.

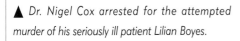
▲ *Dr. Nigel Cox arrested for the attempted murder of his seriously ill patient Lilian Boyes.*

66 *Perhaps now my mother can rest in peace and Dr. Cox can return to the job of treating patients, at which he excels.* 99   *John Boyes, Lilian Boyes' son*

Opponents of euthanasia see the "lenient" treatment of Dr. Cox, and other doctors in a similar position as opening the door for legalization.

66 *We all want death with dignity. But a doctor killing a patient with a lethal injection is acting out of abandonment and despair— not dignity.* 99 *Dr. Robin Bernhoft, heading Washington Physicians Against (Pro-euthanasia) Initiative 119*

One suggested way around the dilemma is to allow assisted suicide to become legal, thereby removing the physical involvement of the doctor. Michigan physician Jack Kevorkian has helped a number of terminally ill patients to commit suicide, and has been acquitted four times of killing through assisted suicide. However, Kevorkian was found guilty of second degree murder in 1999 and sentenced

▲ *Called "Dr. Death" by his opponents, Jack Kevorkian meets the Press with two patients who wish to end their lives with his assistance.*

to 10 to 15 years for assisting the suicide of the terminally ill. Although the state of Oregon allowed assisted suicide in a "death with dignity" act in 1994, for the most part, the medical establishment remains implaccably opposed to the practice.

▶ *Doctors at disasters, such as train crashes, have the dilemma of deciding which of the injured should be treated first.*

A place to die?

There comes a point, when someone is diagnosed as being terminally ill, that their treatment changes. No longer does their doctor seek a cure. Instead, medical staff aim to make the dying patient comfortable. But how effective can they be? Certainly in the case of cancers, and other diseases that can cause great pain, good palliative care—treatment to control pain—is not always available. Neither is a suitable location for dying: most deaths occur in a curtained-off corner of an anonymous hospital ward. This gap—providing excellent palliative care in a caring environment—is one that the hospice movement has strived to fill.

66 This patient-centered philosophy is perhaps what most distinguishes hospices from hospitals, where the disease itself is the focus and the emphasis is on prolonging life rather than dignifying death. Medicine may have failed once a person enters a hospice, but the attitude is no longer one of 'there's nothing more we can do for you.' 99 Kathy Marks, journalist

▲ Dame Cicely Saunders, founder of the hospice movement in Britain, has been a pioneer, with her staff, of the control of pain in dying patients.

▼ Caring for the seriously ill does not necessarily have to take place in a hospice. Community workers can provide care in the patient's home.

Hospice treatment is a holistic approach to medicine. While drugs are used to treat pain, nausea, depression, and other symptoms, hospice staff help the dying patient and their family to come to terms, spiritually and emotionally, with death. In London, a hospice movement was founded in the 1960s by Dame Cicely Saunders, after she witnessed the poor treatment and sidelining of dying patients. Now there are over 250 hospices in Britain and Ireland, and the hospice movement has spread to many countries, including the USA and Canada.

66 I think my wife learnt more of our love during those dreadful months than she did at any other time, and we of hers too.... The suffering of a long and terminal illness is not all waste. Nothing that creates such tenderness can be all waste. 99 Husband speaking of his wife's final months in a hospice

Many, but not all, supporters of the hospice movement are opposed to euthanasia. Apart from finding it morally unacceptable, they suggest that advances in palliative care have removed the need for the patient fearing a painful death.

66 *The hospice, rather than being a 'foot in the door' for euthanasia… can be a powerful force for undercutting a movement for active euthanasia.* 99 *Dame Cicely Saunders*

But many of those who support euthanasia—while praising the aims of the hospice movement—point out its shortcomings. Firstly, there are not enough hospice beds to cope with the number of dying. In Yorkshire in the UK, where hospices are well established, over 40 percent of recent cancer patients died in hospitals, while only 20 percent died in hospices. Secondly, hospices are geared to dealing mainly with deaths from cancer and, in a few cases, from AIDS; other patients suffering from terminal diseases may not receive effective palliative care. Hospice

supporters argue in reply that as more hospices open and as more community workers take hospice care into people's homes, they will be able to provide a comprehensive service for the dying. But does that make euthanasia unnecessary?

▲ *A hospice provides not only for all the needs of the dying patient but for those of her family as well, enabling couples to be close right to the end.*

▼ *A priest visits the sick in St. Joseph's Hospice. Many people find comfort in religion—and some become religious—as their life draws to a close.*

Legal euthanasia?

Should doctors be allowed, by law, to end a patient's life if he or she requests it? This controversial issue is one that will be debated repeatedly as a result of pressure from interested parties, not least the general public—U.S. opinion polls reflect the divisions concerning introducing any euthanasia law.

The arguments against legalizing euthanasia are many: the sanctity of life (see page 8) and the "slippery slope" (see page 12) come high on the list. Doctors might be tempted to abuse their powers and it would be impossible to frame watertight legislation to avoid it.

▼ *The terminally ill often tell their carers that they would like to die quickly and painlessly. Yet do they really want to die or do they simply wish to stop being a burden on their carers?*

66 *We shall start by putting patients away because they are in intolerable pain and haven't long to live anyway; and we shall end up putting them away because it's Friday night and we want to get away for the weekend.* 99 *Doctor's comment quoted by Richard Hare, Professor of Philosophy, University of Florida*

The existence of euthanasia laws might also provide people with an option that they would rather not have.

66 *In a [House of] Commons debate Nicholas Winterton, Conservative MP…said legalizing euthanasia could 'discredit doctors' and put pressure on elderly and chronically sick people who perceived themselves as a burden to relatives.* 99
Doctor magazine, 1995

Supporters of legalizing euthanasia believe that it would give a dying patient control over his or her life by providing a formal procedure to allow its end. It would remove the need for secret euthanasia—by doctors or relatives—which undoubtedly takes place now. Even without government legislation, supporters of voluntary euthanasia and assisted suicide are now finding some support in the courts.

66 *Mentally competent, terminally ill patients have the right to a doctor's assistance in hastening their death, a U.S. federal appeals court ruled…. Judge Stephen Reinhardt said that such a patient has 'a strong liberty interest in choosing a dignified and humane death rather than being reduced at the end of his existence to a childlike state of helplessness, diapered, sedated, incompetent.'* 99
British Medical Journal

In the Netherlands, rather than framing specific laws, voluntary euthanasia is permitted if a strict procedure is followed. Guidelines demand that two doctors diagnose unbearable physical or mental suffering coupled with a persistently expressed desire to die. Some claim that the Dutch system is being abused and that involuntary euthanasia has occurred; others believe that a system of checks and balances

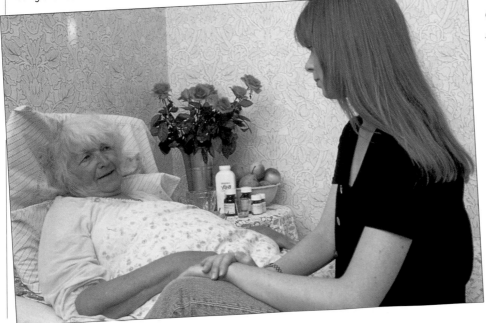

prevents this from happening.

66 *[A Dutch doctor] was fined approximately $35,000 and given a suspended sentence of six months for failing to comply with the official guidelines for voluntary euthanasia. He had ended the life of an incurably ill 63-year-old woman at her request, but he had not consulted with another doctor.... He was barred from practicing medicine.* 99
Voluntary Euthanasia Society Newsletter

Voluntary euthanasia became legal for the first time in the world on July 1, 1996 in Australia's Northern Territory, but was not supported nationally. By March 25, 1997, the law was overturned by the Australian Federal Parliament. While the act was in force, four terminally ill patients died assisted by their doctors.

▲ *Diane Pretty and her husband, Brian, launched legal battles in 2001 and 2002 for her right to die with her husband's help. She was suffering from motor neuron disease. Turned down by British and European courts, she died naturally in May 2002.*

▼ *Lawmaking is a lengthy and complicated process: each law is carefully worded and extensively debated to avoid misinterpretation or abuse. Despite this, many feel it would be impossible to frame watertight laws to legalize euthanasia.*

A life decision?

We are all familiar with the idea of a will. This is a legal document drawn up for someone to direct what will happen to his or her property and money at death. But now there is a variation: a living will or advance directive. This is a written statement given by someone of sound mind to their doctor instructing that his or her life should not be prolonged if they are in the last stages of terminal illness.

❝ *If two independent physicians (one a consultant) are of the opinion that I am unlikely to recover from illness or impairment involving severe distress or incapacity for rational existence.... I am not to be subjected to any medical intervention or treatment aimed at prolonging or sustaining life.* **❞**
Extract from a living will

A living will requests passive, not active, euthanasia under circumstances prescribed by the person whose will it is. In theory, it enables the terminally ill to exert control over their treatment when they are mentally, or physically, no longer able to talk over matters rationally with their doctor or their relatives. It also gives doctors and relatives clear instructions when they have to make decisions on behalf on an "incompetent" patient.

❝ *As a nurse, I've seen the difficult situations people get themselves into. The family and the hospital never know what to do. People are left wondering if they have made the right decision. This way, the onus falls on me.* **❞**
Shane Snape, AIDS sufferer who completed a living will

A patient who has made a living will and develops a terminal illness can ask to be given painkillers to relieve distressing symptoms, but not to be prescribed antibiotic drugs that would prolong life. Living wills are now recognized in all U.S. states and, though not tested in the courts, increasingly in other countries.

❝ *Contrary to what some have tried to assert, an advance directive is not a move toward legalising euthanasia. It is a way for patients to exercise their right to refuse treatment by anticipating a time when they may lose the capacity to make or convey the decision.* **❞**
Tony Blair, British Prime Minister, 1997

▶ *A living will allows people to make decisions about their life—and death—in advance in case they succumb, like these two women, to diseases such as Alzheimer's that affect their competence.*

77 percent of Americans aged 65–74 and 74 percent aged 18 and older considered living wills very important. But only an estimated 20–30 percent of Americans are believed to have made living wills.

◀ *Patients who have firm ideas about how they would wish to be treated in case of severe illness should discuss their feelings with their doctor.*

▼ *Writing a living will is not unlike the common practice of carrying a donor card, which instructs the donation of body organs, such as the kidneys, to other people in the event of your death.*

But there is opposition to living wills,.especially from those who oppose euthanasia—patients have no right to choose when they die and nor do their doctors.

66 *Living wills threaten lives. They enable doctors to end the lives of patients, while protecting the doctor from civil or criminal liability.* **99** *Information from ALERT, an anti-euthanasia organization*

Others also add that living wills could be abused to save money.

66 *Living wills…can be a tool in the hands of those who want to cut the costs of looking after the handicapped, cut the costs of looking after the terminally ill.* **99** *Paul Tully, of the Society for the Protection of the Unborn Child*

It appears, however, that living wills will be increasingly accepted by the medical profession. The question is: will people actually make such wills? A 2002 U.S. survey found that

LIVING WILL

To my family, my physician, and all other persons concerned this living will is made by me SARAH SMITH of 20 PARK CRESCENT, TOWNLY at a time when I am of sound mind and after careful consideration.

I DECLARE that if at any time the following circumstances exists, namely:

(1) I suffer from one or more of the conditi mentioned bel and have be participa

ORGAN DONOR CARD
I would like to help someone to live after my death.

Let your relatives know your wishes, and keep this card with you at all times.

Death with dignity?

How dignified can death be? Is it a natural thing for people who are dying to experience some pain and suffering in their last days?

66 *According to Christian teaching, suffering, especially during the last moments of life, has a special place in God's saving plan. It is in fact a sharing in Christ's Passion and a union with the redeeming sacrifice which He offered in obedience to the Father's will.* 99 The Vatican's Declaration on Euthanasia, 1980

Or should life end, whenever possible, in a calm, peaceful, and dignified manner? And if necessary through euthanasia?

▼ *Visiting the sick and dying at home used to be a normal part of life, as this 19th-century engraving shows.*

▲ Captain Oates, part of Scott's ill-fated 1912 polar expedition, sought a quick end in a blizzard rather than burden his comrades when he fell ill.

66 *Death has dominion because it is not only the start of nothing but the end of everything, and how we think and talk about dying—the emphasis we put on dying with 'dignity'—shows how important it is that life ends appropriately, that death keeps faith with the way we have lived.* 99
Ronald Dworkin, Life's Dominion

There are no easy answers to these questions. Death is a stranger to most of us, and we

have no practical experience of it, although we may fear the pain of dying and the loss of loved ones. Today, we are more likely to delegate responsibility for caring for the dying to the medical profession, and by so doing, perhaps lose the opportunity to give ourselves or our relatives a dignified departure. In the USA, 80 percent of deaths take place in

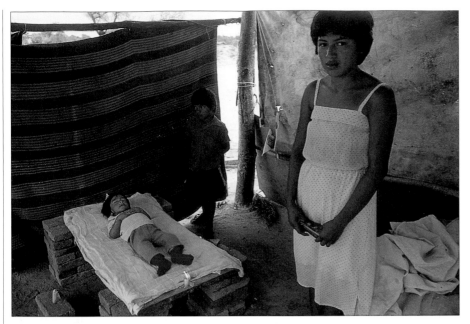

▲ A mother stands by her dead child in her home in Bolivia. In developing countries, death continues to be a part of "everyday" life.

own way for their own death or that of their relatives. Should we redefine our understanding of death in order to accommodate it with all the other aspects of our life?

66 *A natural death center, offering midwives for the dying, death exercises, recyclable coffins, and a do-it-yourself guide to getting bodies to graveyards, [has opened] in London. Nicholas Albery, the founder, says his idea came from natural childbirth. 'There could be that same feeling of expectation, of transition, as at birth. Dying could be an ecstatic experience.'* **99**
The Guardian newspaper

hospitals; in Britain the figure is over 75 percent. But should control over the way a person dies be taken away from her or him because of improved medical services?

66 *There should be societies for home deaths. Being looked after at home is more trouble, of course, just as home cooking takes more time. But dying in a hospital as most people now do, stuck full of tubes in white rooms, surrounded by suffering and strangers, with those you love kept at the end of a telephone, is a sad and bad ending. Caroline thought that being sent to hospital to die was like being put on a dumpster... Caroline took responsibility for her death, simply by stopping eating, two weeks before she died.* **99**
Geoffrey Cannon, remembering his wife, Caroline Walker, who died from cancer

There are moves in the USA, UK, and other countries to establish organizations that can make death, once again, an everyday part of life, and to help people prepare in their

▼ These Texans belong to the "Snowbirds," a group of older men and women dedicated to enjoying life and making the most of the years that remain before they die.

Which funeral?

It seems perfectly normal to most people that if and when relatives or friends die they ask a funeral director to arrange the funeral or cremation. But some people are now questioning the whole "machinery" of death and funerals in the developed world. Why should they hand over their loved one's body to strangers after she or he has died for a funeral that is not to their liking?

66 *Within a century, we have swung away from showy funerals that went way over the top in displaying social status, to plastic funerals that say nothing, that say the person was nothing … A funeral provides an opportunity to mark the passing of a human life. All too often we waste this opportunity.* **99** *Tony Walter, Funerals and How to Improve Them*

Certainly, the funeral business has sometimes appeared to be more concerned with making money than

providing a caring farewell to the dead. There is a growing trend, too, for funeral parlors to be absorbed into large multinational companies that can be thought to provide a fairly impersonal "funeral package." In response to this trend, there are several movements that seek to improve the lot of the dead and their relatives.

▲ *The nature of funerals worldwide varies greatly. For example, this Akan funeral in Ghana, typically noisy with rhythmic beating of drums, contrasts strongly with the quieter and more gloomy atmosphere of a standard British funeral.*

▼ *In the 18th century, British funerals were often elaborate and ostentatious. The amount of pomp and the number of carriages would be a reflection of the wealth and status of the recently deceased.*

> A 'Dead Citizen's Charter' aimed at transforming funerals from an often short and impersonal experience into an occasion that honors the dead and lets friends and relatives mourn properly, is to be launched today.
> *The Independent newspaper, 1996*

Centers exist that, among other services, provide help and encouragement to people who want to buy their own coffins—sometimes highly decorated ones—off the shelf, arrange the venue and nature of the funeral service, and even find a plot

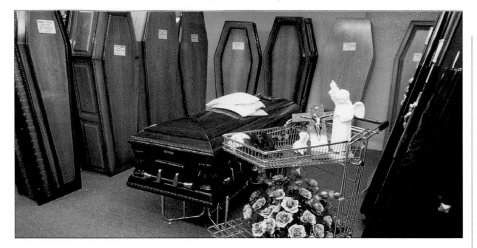

of their choice for burial. Some people find arranging the funeral before you die can help both you and your relatives prepare for death.

> *Planning the funeral ourselves and discussing it with his grown-up children helped us all to come to terms with his approaching death.*
> *Sheila Page, describing organizing his funeral with her terminally ill husband before he died*

Many funeral directors defend their role by saying that they provide an efficient, cost-effective service for people at a time when they are grieving and unable to carry out all the arrangements for a funeral themselves. Some are quite hostile to the new trends.

> *A truly terrible idea. When you think of the small amount of timber that would be saved, the ecological benefit would be infinitesimal. The trauma of seeing our nearest and dearest buried in a body bag far outweighs any good that might have been done.*
> *Walter Parsons, the National Association of Funeral Directors, commenting on recyclable coffins*

▲ A recent innovation, the funeral supermarket offers a selection of ready-made coffins and accessories at a lower price than funeral directors.

But some funeral directors are now happy to cooperate flexibly with families in helping to arrange funerals that suit their individual needs, and which allow them to say a personal farewell to a loved one. This may, or may not, be a trend that continues, depending on how much our attitudes to death change in the future.

▼ This ox-shaped coffin contains a body on its way to a cremation ceremony on the Indonesian island of Bali.

▼ Few of us would choose to buy our coffins in advance. Perhaps this coffin, which can be used as a bookcase, might change our minds.

A right to live?

There is no doubt that advances in medicine have given some patients, who would previously have died, the chance to live longer lives. But should these opportunities for life extension be available for all people, regardless of their circumstances?

In the case of kidney dialysis machines, for example, there may be more patients than machines; doctors have to decide which patients are most "deserving," but what criteria for choice should they employ? As a further example, the state of Oregon has adopted a controversial rationing system for those receiving free medical treatment: a tight budget has forced it to limit care based on how much treatment will cost and how effective it will be. Further concerns have been raised by the suggestion to legalize assisted suicide in the state.

❝My medical services providers will be faced with a choice between treating me at reduced charge or denying me treatment altogether.... I am concerned that they will subject me to undue influence or duress to end my life in order to enable them to avoid that dilemma. ❞
Eric Dutson, AIDS sufferer in Oregon

In the UK in 2003, Sarah Kemp told the BBC she had made a full recovery three years after her parents refused permission to turn off her life support machine. Sarah, then 20, had been in a riding accident in 1999 in which her horse fell on her. Doctors warned that she would be brain damaged if she came out of the coma, and they gave her a 10 percent chance of survival. After her parents refused, Sarah awoke from her seven-week coma and began to recover.

❝My family were asked to turn off the life support machine so that shows how bad it was.... Doctors can't believe how amazing my recovery has been. I'm really chuffed. ❞ Sarah Kemp

It is a harsh fact that in most countries no one has an absolute right to life-saving treatment. Medical care is expensive: is it right to stay within budgets and make health care available to those most likely to survive? Does this make euthanasia an easier option because it removes

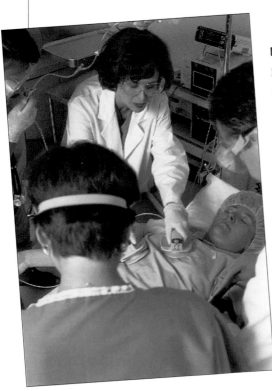

▼ A crash team resuscitates a patient after her heart stops. Resuscitation may not be attempted if doctors feel it is not in the patient's best interest.

▶ Sarah Kemp from Kidderminster, England, awoke from a coma after hearing her dad tell her to hurry up and get out for her 21st birthday, which was just two weeks away.

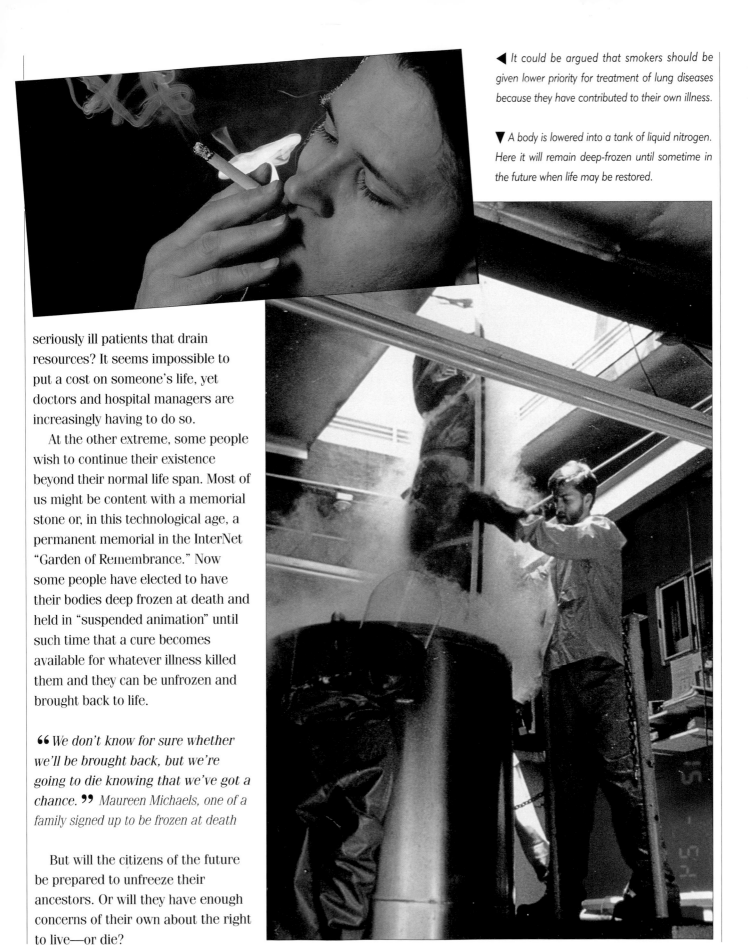

seriously ill patients that drain resources? It seems impossible to put a cost on someone's life, yet doctors and hospital managers are increasingly having to do so.

At the other extreme, some people wish to continue their existence beyond their normal life span. Most of us might be content with a memorial stone or, in this technological age, a permanent memorial in the InterNet "Garden of Remembrance." Now some people have elected to have their bodies deep frozen at death and held in "suspended animation" until such time that a cure becomes available for whatever illness killed them and they can be unfrozen and brought back to life.

66 *We don't know for sure whether we'll be brought back, but we're going to die knowing that we've got a chance.* **99** *Maureen Michaels, one of a family signed up to be frozen at death*

But will the citizens of the future be prepared to unfreeze their ancestors. Or will they have enough concerns of their own about the right to live—or die?

Glossary

AIDS (ACQUIRED IMMUNE DEFICIENCY SYNDROME): An incurable condition in which a virus (HIV) weakens the body's natural defense system leaving the body open to infection by potentially fatal diseases.

ALZHEIMER'S DISEASE: A progressive brain disease, usually in old age, which causes loss of mental abilities.

ANATHEMA: Something which a person detests or finds unacceptable.

ASSISTED SUICIDE: A form of *euthanasia* in which a person is given access to the means to kill him or herself by a doctor or other person.

CANCER: One of a group of diseases (such as lung cancer) in which certain body cells multiply out of control to form a tumor and eventually, if not treated in time, spread throughout the body and kill the patient.

CHRIST'S PASSION: The sufferings of Jesus Christ on the Cross.

CRIMINAL LIABILITY: An obligation to behave according to the law or otherwise be prosecuted for committing a crime.

EUTHANASIA: The act of ending someone's life painlessly, usually to relieve incurable suffering.

HOSPICE: A small hospital or home dedicated to caring for the terminally ill, including provision of pain relief.

INELIMINABLE: Describes something that cannot be destroyed or eliminated.

INTRINSIC: Describes something that is an essential part of something else.

LEGAL: Describes something connected with, or carried out according to, the law.

LEGISLATION: A law or laws.

LEGISLATURE: An assembly, such as the U.S. Congress, which makes laws.

LIVING WILL: A personal document that describes how a person would wish to be treated by doctors and carers if he or she become mentally or physically unable to discuss matters.

MOTOR NEURON DISEASE (MND): A progressive disease that leads to weakness and wasting of muscles, leaving the sufferer immobilized.

NAZI: Describes a member of, or anything to do with, the National Socialist Party which, under Adolf Hitler, ruled Germany between 1933 and the end of World War II in 1945.

PALLIATIVE CARE: Treatment to relieve the severe pain and other symptoms that dying patients may experience.

PASSIVE EUTHANASIA: Withdrawal of medical treatment or a life support system resulting in a patient's death.

PERSISTENT VEGETATIVE STATE (PVS): Deep coma, caused by brain damage, from which patients may not recover.

PHYSICIAN: Another name for a doctor.

ROMAN CATHOLIC CHURCH: The branch of Christianity, led by the Pope in Rome, with the largest following worldwide.

SANCTITY: The quality of something being sacred and morally pure.

SECULAR: Describes something that is not concerned with religious matters.

SUICIDE: Killing oneself intentionally.

TABOO: Something that is forbidden, banned, or not acknowledged.

TEMPORAL: Relating to the time we are alive on Earth.

TERMINAL: At the end, final.

VOLUNTARY EUTHANASIA: Giving a severely ill patient, at their request, a lethal substance to end their life.

Useful addresses

American Civil Liberties Union
125 Broad Street,
New York, NY 10004
www.aclu.org

Canadian Civil Liberties Association
Suite 200, 394 Bloor Street West
Toronto, ON M5S 1X4
www.ccla.org

Choices in Dying
Box 79521
Vancouver, BC
Canada
www.choicesindying@shaw.ca

Center for Human Rights Education
P.O. Box 311020
Atlanta, GA 31311
www.accessatlanta.com/community/
groups/chre/

Compassion in Dying
6312 SW Capitol Hwy
Suite 415
Portland, OR 97201
www.compassionindying.org

The Council of Canadians
502-151 Slater St.
Ottawa, Ontario, K1P 5H3
Canada
www.canadians.org

End-of-Life Choices
PO Box 101810
Denver, CO 80250
www.endollifechoices.org

Euthanasia Research and Guidance
Organization
24829 Norris Lane
Junction City, OR 97448
www.finalexit.org

Life Issues Institute
1821 W. Galbraith Rd.
Cincinatti, OH 45239
www.lifeissuesinstitute.o

Facts to think about

◆ While death may be an inevitable part of life, surveys have revealed that 90 percent of 19-year-olds never consider death in relation to themselves, while 70 percent of 65-year-olds do.

◆ The average life expectancy in the USA is currently about 75 for men and 80 for women. However, a man who has reached the age of 65 can expect, on average, to live until he is 80 and a 60-year-old woman to

◆ The two major causes of death among men and women in most western countries are circulatory system diseases (including heart attacks and strokes) and cancers.

◆ In USA, more than 6,000 people commit suicide each year.

◆ In the Netherlands 1,882 cases of legal voluntary euthanasia were recorded in 2002, a drop of 15 percent over four year.

◆ A 2003 poll found that almost 75 percent of 986 a selected group of doctors surveyed would refuse to participate in an assisted suicide, and 56 percent felt it is impossible to set safe limits.

◆ In 1995 the British Medical Association (BMA) recognized the validity of living wills.

◆ In the USA, a conventional funeral arranged by a funeral director costs on average around $7000.

Index